WAY OF RHEA
AMIGURUMI

By: K. Whitmeyer

TABLE OF CONTENTS

ABOUT THIS BOOK

Creature is solving puzzles to help his friends. Shrew is riding on his motorcycle and poor Hermie is always getting lost. The adorable amigurumi pieces shown in this book are inspired by the Way of Rhea game. Way of Rhea is an indie game that is full of vibrant worlds and challenging puzzles. This crochet book is a fan made instructional guide that allows you to bring the whimsical characters in the game to life.

— **Kristina Whitmeyer**

ABBREVIATIONS / RESOURCES

Ch:	Chain
St:	Stich
R:	Round
Sc:	single crochet
Inc:	increase
Dec:	decrease
Sl St:	Slip Stich
X # :	Repeat the number of times (For example: x6 is <u>repeat 6 times</u>)
[#] :	total number of stiches for the round (For example: [24] is 24 stiches

Resources

- YouTube Tutorials - @Mrs.WhitmeyersCrochetCreations
- Way of Rhea Game- Can be purchased on Steam

CREATURE

(<u>Skill level</u>- Advance)

<u>Materials</u>

- Crochet hook 5mm
- Crochet stopper
- Blue yarn (5mm)
- Pink yarn (5mm)
- Hot glue gun
- White felt
- Black felt
- Stuffing
- Sticks
- Stich marker
- Crochet needle
- Gray Faux fox fur

CREATURE

Body (blue yarn)

- R1: ch 6 in magic ring [6]
- R2: inc all 6 [12]
- R3: (sc, inc) X 6 [18]
- R4: (2 sc, inc) X 6 [24]
- R5: (3sc, inc) x6 [30]
- R6: (4sc, inc) x 6 [36]
- R7: (5sc, inc) x 6 [42]
- R8: (6sc, inc) x 6 [48]
- R 9- R17: (sc) x 8 [48]
- R18: (6sc, dec) [48]
- R19: (5sc, dec) [42]
- R20: (4sc, dec) [36]
- R21: (3sc, dec) [30]
- R22: (2sc, dec) [24]
- (Add stuffing)
- R23: (sc, dec) [18]
- R24: dec [12]

Tail

- R1: Ch 10 [10]
- R2: sc in the top loop moving towards the left
- R3: sl st through the top loop and very bottom loop,

Arms & Legs (Total of 4)

- R1- ch 5 in magic ring [5]
- R2- inc all 5 [10]
- R3- R10 (sc) x 7 [10]

ASSEMBLY

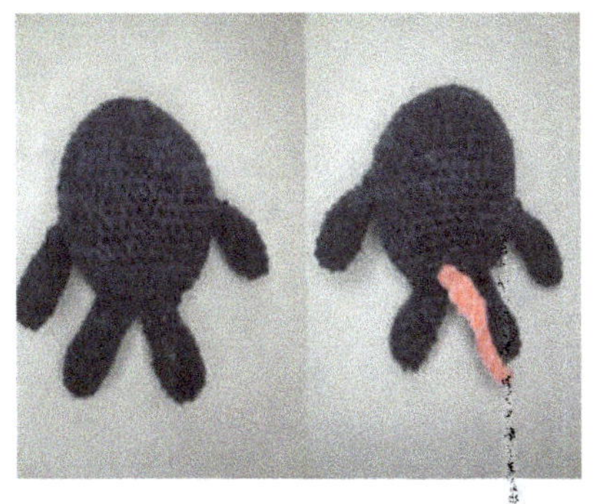

1 Sew arms, legs, and tail

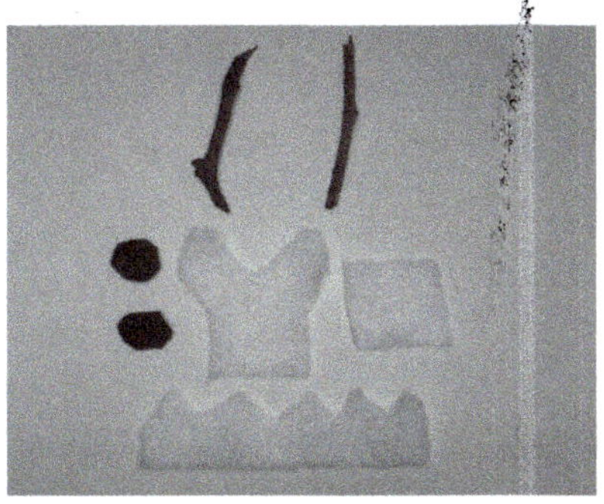

2 Cut out the parts of the mask from the black and white felt

3 Glue parts of the mask together

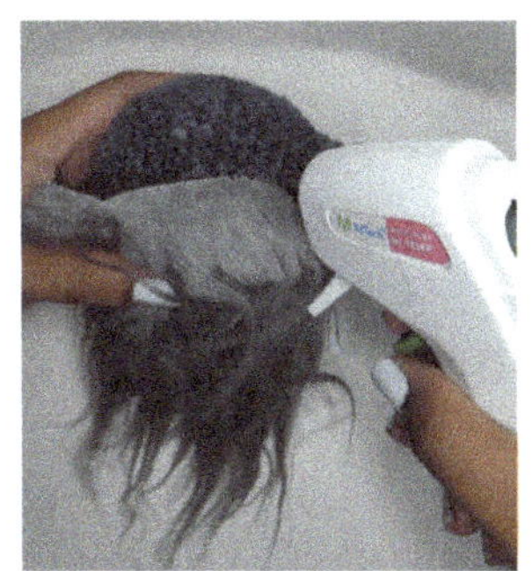

4 Cut faux fur into strips and glue onto body. Start at the top of the body and glue all sections.

5 Brush down faux fur and glue on mask

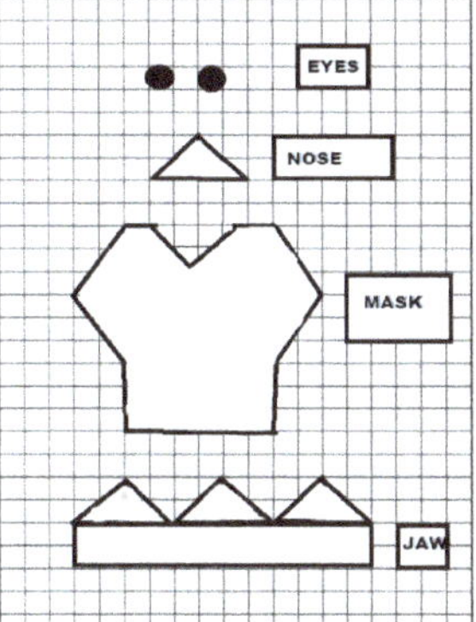

Template for Mask

HERMIE

(<u>Skill level</u>- Medium)

Materials

- Crochet hook 5mm

- Dark blue yarn (5mm)

- Green yarn (5mm)

- Hot glue gun

- 2 black buttons

- Crochet stopper

- Stuffing

- Crochet needle

HERMIE

Belly (Bottom section- dark blue yarn)

- R1: ch 6 in magic ring [6]
- R2: inc all 6 [12]
- R3: (sc, inc) X 6 [18]
- R4: (2 sc, inc) X 6 [24]
- R5: (3sc, inc) x6 [30]
- R6: (4sc, inc) x 6 [36]
- R7: (5sc, inc) x 6 [42]
- R8: (6sc, inc) x 6 [48]
- R 9- R14: (sc) x 5 [48]

Spikes (5 total) (green)

- R1: ch 4 in magic ring [4] R5: (sc) [12]
- R2: (sc, inc) X 4 [8]
- R3: (sc) [8]
- R4: (2 sc, inc) X 4 [12]

Top Shell (Green yarn)

- R1: ch 6 in magic ring [6]
- R2: inc all 6 [12]
- R3: (sc, inc) X 6 [18]
- R4: (2 sc, inc) X 6 [24]
- R5: (3sc, inc) x6 [30]
- R6: (4sc, inc) x 6 [36]
- R7: (5sc, inc) x 6 [42]
- R8: (6sc, inc) x 6 [48]
- R 9: inc in all st [48]

Arms (4 total)

- R1: ch 4 in magic ring [4]
- R2: inc all 4 [8]
- R3- R7: (sc) X 5 [8]

❶ Sew Belly and Top shell together. Add stuffing before you completely sew it shut.

❷ Add stuffing to legs and spikes. Sew them onto the body with a crochet needle

❸ Glue buttons for eyes on the belly potion

SHREW

(<u>Skill level</u>- Beginner)

Materials

- Crochet hook 4 mm
- Brown yarn (4 mm)
- Black Yarn/ string
- Hot glue gun
- Black felt
- White felt
- Hot glue gun
- Crochet stopper
- Stuffing
- Crochet needle

Shrew

SHREW

Head

- R1: ch 6 in magic ring [6]
- R2: inc all 6 [12]
- R3: (sc, inc) X 6 [18]
- R4: (sc) [18]
- R5: (5sc, inc) x6 [18]
- R6- R8: (SC) x 6 [21]
- R9: (5sc, dec) x 6 [21]
- R10: (sc, dec) x 6 [18]
- (Add Stuffing)
- R 11: (dec) x 6 [12]

Snout

- R1: ch 4 in magic ring [4]
- R2: (sc, inc) X 4 [8]
- R3: (sc) X 4 [8]
- R4: (sc, inc) x4 [12]
- R5: (2sc, inc) x4 [18]

Ears (2 total)

- R1: ch 2
- R2: 4 sc into the first chain
- R3: ch 1
- R4: Sl st
- R5: (sc) [18]

Legs and Arms (4 total)

- R1: ch 5 in magic ring [5]
- R2- R4: (sc) x 4 [5]

Body

- R1: ch 5 in magic ring [5]
- R2: inc all 5 [10]
- R3: (sc, inc) X 5 [15]
- R4: (2 sc, inc) X 5 [20]
- R5: (3sc, inc) x 5 [25]
- R6: (4sc, inc) x 5 [30]
- R7- R9: (sc) x 2 [30]
- R10: (4sc, dec) x 5 [30]
- R 11: (3sc, dec) x 5 [25]
- R12: (2sc, dec) x 5 [20]
- R13: (sc, dec) x5 [15] (Add Stuffing)
- R14: (dec) x5 [10]

ASSEMBLY

1 Sew ears and snout to the head with a crochet needle. Sew arms and legs to the body. Sew head

2 Cut out the parts of the mask from the black and white felt.

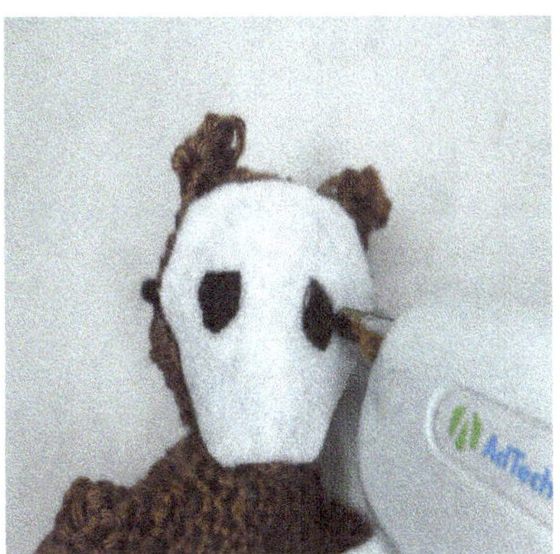

3 Glue parts of mask together and place on face of Shrew.

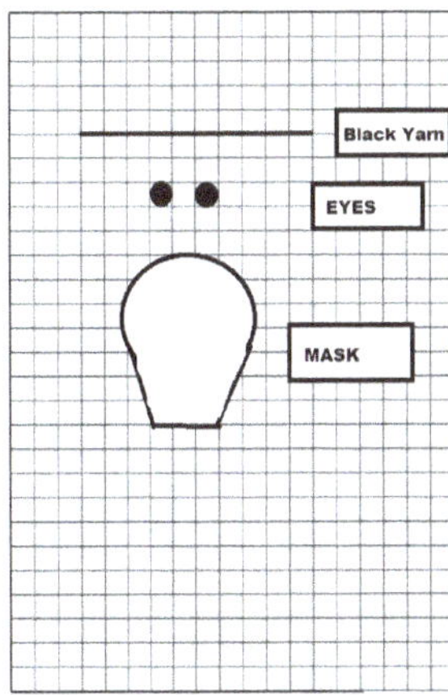

Template for Mask

PAPA SNOW CRAB

(<u>Skill level</u>- Medium)

Materials

- Crochet hook 5mm
- Dark blue yarn (5mm)
- Green yarn (5mm)
- Hot glue gun
- 2 black buttons
- Crochet stopper
- Stuffing
- Crochet needle

PAPA SNOW CRAB

Main shell (green)

- R1: ch 6 in magic ring [6]
- R2: inc all 6 [12]
- R3: (sc, inc) X 6 [18]
- R4: (2 sc, inc) X 6 [24]
- R5: (3sc, inc) x6 [30]
- R6: (4sc, inc) x 6 [36]
- R7: (5sc, inc) x 6 [42]
- R8: (6sc, inc) x 6 [48]
- R 9: (7sc, inc) x 6 [56]
- R 10: (8sc, inc) x 6 [64]
- R11- R13: (sc) [64]

Mini spines (green x5)

- R1: ch 6 in magic ring [6]
- R2: (sc) [6]
- R3: increase in all 6 [12]
- R4: (sc) [12]
- R5: increase in all 12 [24]
- R6: (sc) [24]

Mini spines (green x5)

- R1: ch 4 in magic ring [4]
- R2: (sc) [4]
- R3: increase in all 4 [8]
- R4: (sc) [8]

Bottom shell (dark blue)

- R1: ch 6 in magic ring [6]
- R2: inc all 6 [12]
- R3: (sc, inc) X 6 [18]
- R4: (2 sc, inc) X 6 [24]
- R5: (3sc, inc) x6 [30]
- R6: (4sc, inc) x 6 [36]
- R7: (5sc, inc) x 6 [42]
- R8: (6sc, inc) x 6 [48]
- R 9: (7sc, inc) x 6 [56]
- R 10- R11: (sc) [56]

Legs (dark blue x4)

- R1: ch 4 in magic ring [4]
- R2: inc all 4 [8]
- R3-R8: (sc) [8]

ASSEMBLY

1 Sew main shell to bottom shell. onto body.

2 Sew on main in the center and add stuffing as needed. Sew on mini spikes

3 Sew on legs

4 Use hot glue gun to attach eyes

THE PROFESSOR

(<u>Skill level</u>- Advance)

Materials

- Crochet hook 5mm
- Crochet stopper
- White yarn (5mm)
- Gold felt
- Hot glue gun
- black felt
- purple felt
- Stuffing
- Crochet needle
- Scissors

PROFESSOR

Head (white yarn)

- R1: ch 6 in magic ring [6]
- R2: inc all 6 [12]
- R3: (sc, inc) X 6 [18]
- R4: (2 sc, inc) X 6 [24]
- R5: (3sc, inc) x6 [30]
- R6: (4sc, inc) x 6 [36]
- R7- R15: (sc) x 6 [36]
- R16: (4sc, dec) x 6 [30]
- R 17: (3sc, dec) x 8 [24]
- R18: (2sc, dec) [18]
- R19: (sc, dec) [12]
- R20: (dec) [6]

Snout

- R1: ch 6 in magic ring [6]
- R2: inc all 6 [12]
- R3: (sc) X 6 [12]
- R4: (3 sc, inc) X 6 [18]
- R5-6: (sc) x6 [18]
- R7: (4sc, inc) x 6 [24]
- R8- R9: (sc) x 6 [24]

Body

- R1: ch 6 in magic ring [6]
- R2: inc all 6 [12]
- R3-R7: (sc) X 6 [12]
- (first leg- fasten)
- R8: ch 6 in magic ring [6]
- R9: inc all 6 [12]
- R10-R15: (sc) X 6 [12]
- (second leg- sew together)
- R16- R23: (sc) X 6 [24]
- R24: (2sc, dec) x 6 [18]
- R25: (sc) x 6 [18]
- R26: (sc, dec) x 6 [12]
- R 27: (dec) x 6 [6]

Hat

- R1: ch 6 in magic ring [6]
- R2: inc all 6 [12]
- R3: (sc, inc) X 6 [18]
- R4: (2 sc, inc) X 6 [24]
- R5-R6: (sc) x6 [18]

Arms

- (start with gray)
- R1: ch 6 in magic ring [6]
- R2: (sc, inc) [12]
- (Fasten gray string and switch to white)
- R3-8: (sc) X 6 [12]

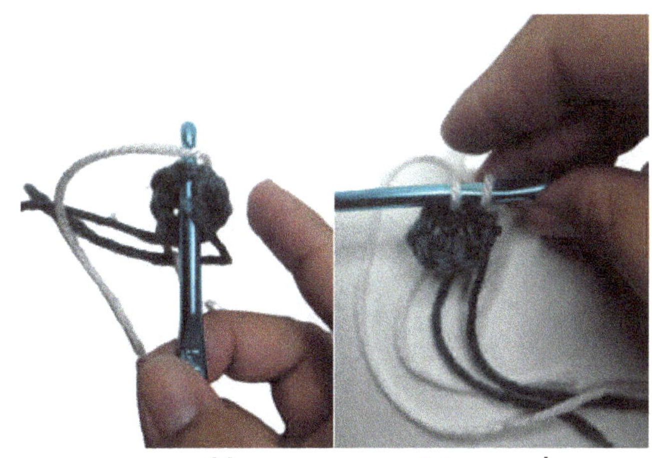

How to transition colors
from gray to white on

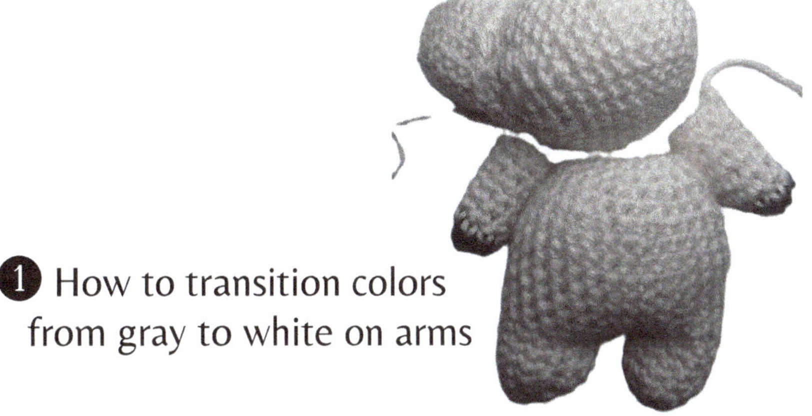

❶ How to transition colors
from gray to white on arms

2 Glue purple felt like a cape

3 H Trim front exposing hands

4 Cut front portion and glue

4 Cut out shapes from using the template and use them to design the professor's clothes.

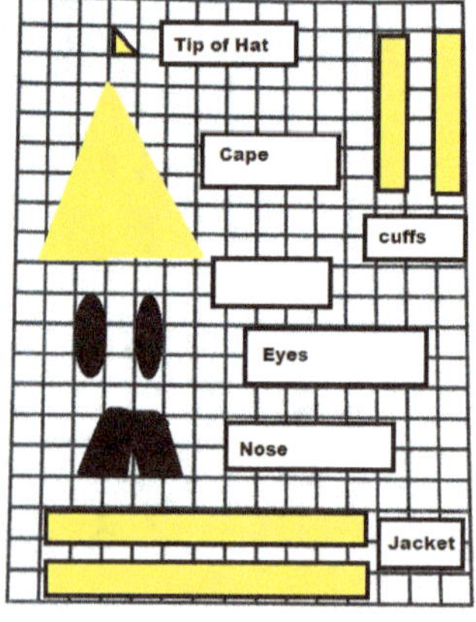

Template

RHEA

Materials

- Crochet hook 5mm
- Crochet stopper
- Black yarn (5mm)
- Hot glue gun
- White felt
- Black felt
- Stuffing
- Crochet needle
- Black sharpie
- Red sharpie

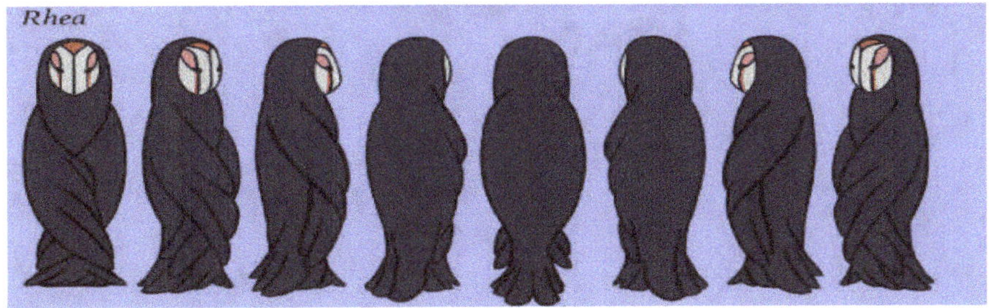

RHEA

Wings X2

- R1: ch 6 in magic ring [6]
- R2: (2sc, inc) X6 [12]
- R3: (3sc, inc) X 6 [18]
- R4: ch 7 in ring [6]
- R5: (2sc, inc) x6 [12]
- R6: (3sc, inc) x 6 [18]
- R7: ch 7 in ring [6]
- R8: (2sc, inc) x 6 [12]
- R 9: (3sc, inc) x 6 [18]
- R 10: (sc) connecting all three parts of the wing [60]
- R11: (3sc, dec) X 6 [42]
- R12: (sc) X 6 [42]
- R13: (2sc, dec) x6 [24]
- R14: (sc) x 6 [24]
- R15: (sc, dec) x 6 [6]
- R16: (sc) x 6 [6]
- R17: (dec) x6

Body

- Body
- R1: ch 6 in magic ring [6]
- R2: inc all 6 [12]
- R3: (sc, inc) X 6 [18]
- R4: (2sc, inc) x6 [24]
- R5- R8: (sc) x6 [24]
- R9: (2sc, dec) x 6 [18]
- R10: (sc, dec) X6 [12]
- R11: (dec) x 6 [6]
- R 12-R14: (sc) x 6 [6]
- R 15: (sc, inc) X 6 [12]
- R16- R25: (sc) X 6 [12]
- R26: (sc, dec) X6 [6]
- R27: (dec) x6

ASSEMBLY

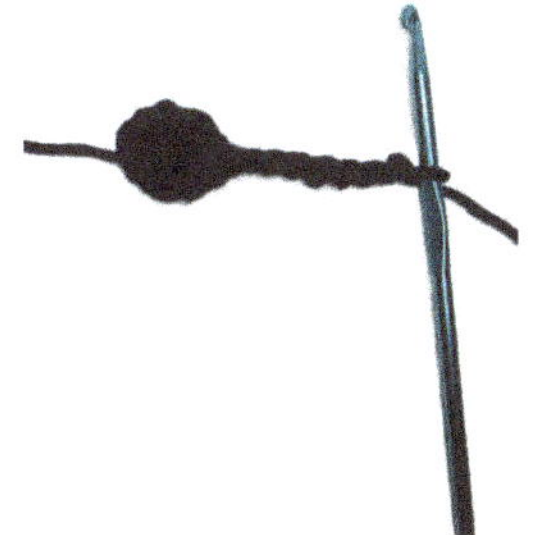

Visual of Round 4

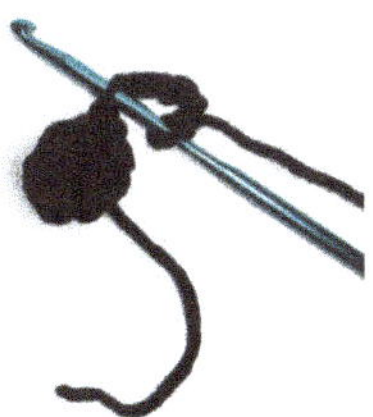

Visual of Round 4 forming a ring and then start round 5

Visual of round 10

1 Crochet wings and Body

2 Shape Head

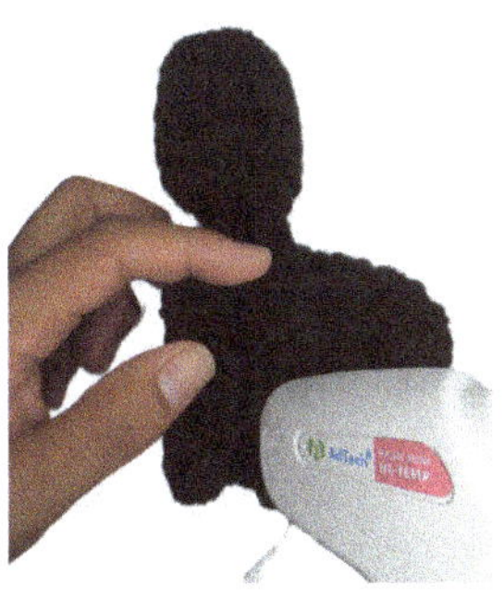

3 Wrap wings around body and glue into place

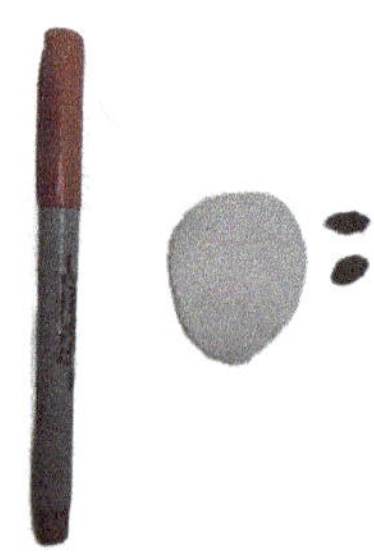

4 Wrap wings around body and glue into place

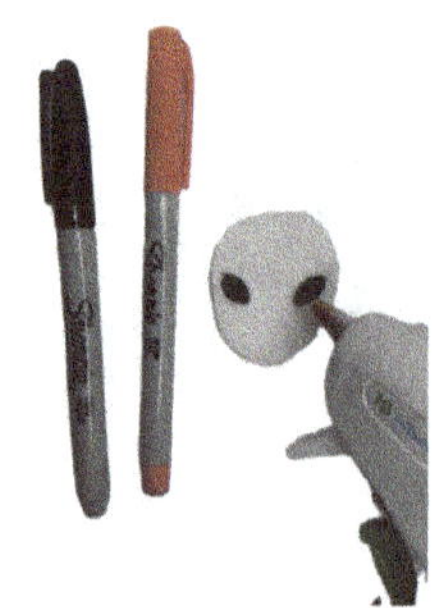

5 Wrap wings around body and glue into place

6 Wrap wings around body and glue into place

7 Glue on mask

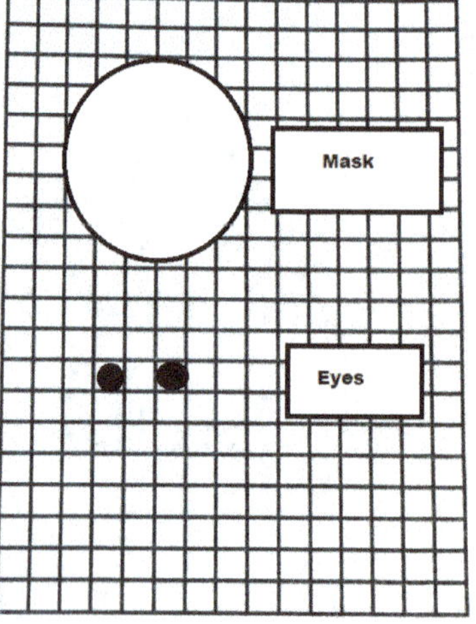

Mask Template

Grab your crochet hook and dive into Rhea's magnificent world. Way of Rhea is an indie game that is full of fascinating biomes and unique characters. This crochet book is a fan made instructional guide that allows you to bring the adorable characters in the game to life. Make your own plushies by following the crochet patterns in this book.